Accepted and Free

BREAKING THE POWER
OF REJECTION

TOM CORNELL

ACCEPTED AND FREE

BREAKING THE POWER OF REJECTION

TOM CORNELL

SOZO PUBLISHING

Paperback ISBN: 978-1-969882-04-3

CONTENTS

INTRODUCTION
REJECTION'S SILENT STRONGHOLD

Rejection is one of the most subtle, yet spiritually lethal weapons the enemy uses to keep God's sons and daughters in bondage. It rarely walks through the front door wearing a name tag. Instead, it disguises itself as fear, shame, insecurity, perfectionism, control, passivity, and striving. It hides behind personality quirks, unhealthy patterns, and deep emotional wounds. While it may begin as a feeling, it eventually becomes a lens—a filter that distorts how we see ourselves, others, and even God.

You don't have to look far to find rejection's fingerprints. It shows up in the silent pain of a child who longs for a father's approval but only receives criticism. It echoes in the heart of a teenager excluded by peers, unsure if they'll ever belong. It hardens into bitterness in the wife who feels unseen, or the husband who feels he'll never measure up. It festers in the pastor's soul after church hurt, in the employee passed over for promotion, and in the friend who always feels one step outside the circle. Rejection isn't just an occasional wound—it's a strategy from hell to disconnect us from love, distort our identity, and keep us from walking in our divine destiny. But here's the good news: Jesus was rejected so you could be accepted.

The cross wasn't just the payment for your sin; it was the ultimate confrontation with every form of rejection mankind has ever known. Jesus was despised, betrayed, denied, falsely accused, mocked, abandoned, and crucified outside the camp. Every type of human rejection was laid upon Him. Why? So you could be embraced by the Father. So you could be healed from every wound. So you could walk in the Spirit of adoption, no longer an orphan, but a beloved son or daughter.

Yet even many believers—those who are saved, filled with the Spirit, and active in church—still carry the residue of rejection. They serve while secretly striving. They lead while silently questioning their worth. They pray but still feel like outsiders in the Father's house. Rejection doesn't just keep people from salvation—it keeps Christians from intimacy, freedom, and fruitfulness.

This book is for the hidden places. It's for those who've managed their pain long enough. It's for the people who outwardly seem strong, but inwardly feel unworthy, unnoticed, or unloved. It's for those who crave closeness but push people away. It's for those who work harder, try more, and perform better—but still wonder, "Do I really belong?"

Over the next three sections, we will walk through a healing journey—a process of uncovering, uprooting, and overcoming.

- In Part One, we will expose the many faces of rejection, how it enters, what it partners with, and how it manifests in a person's life.

- In Part Two, we will dive deep into inner healing, forgiveness, and deliverance—giving you tools and Spirit-led strategies to be truly free.
- In Part Three, we will show you how to walk as one who is deeply loved, accepted, and secure. No more hiding. No more striving. No more spiritual guessing games.

You were not created to live in fear of rejection. You were born for belonging. You were not made to perform for love—you were made to live from love. Your story is not one of abandonment, but adoption. You are not on the outside looking in—you are seated at the table.

This is not just a book. It's an invitation—to healing, to wholeness, and to walking boldly in your true identity. The Father is calling His sons and daughters home, not just into Heaven, but into His heart. It's time to stop surviving rejection and start living accepted and free.

PART I

THE ROOTS AND FRUITS
OF REJECTION

THE MANY FACES OF REJECTION

*R*ejection is one of the most universal human experiences—and one of the most misunderstood. It's more than an emotional sting or social setback. It's a force that wounds the soul, distorts identity, and opens the door to spiritual bondage if left unhealed. Rejection doesn't look the same in every person. Sometimes it screams in anger, sometimes it hides in silence. Sometimes it produces isolation, and other times it manifests as obsessive people-pleasing. But in every case, rejection leaves the heart questioning its value and fighting for belonging.

This chapter will help you recognize how rejection shows up in your story—because you can't heal what you haven't identified.

What Rejection Really Is

Rejection is the experience—or perception—of being unwanted, unloved, unworthy, or excluded. Sometimes it comes through real, overt actions. Other times, it's the quiet result of emotional neglect or unintentional harm. Rejection says: "You don't belong. You're not enough. You're not wanted."

It isn't just a passing emotion—it becomes a root issue that feeds other spiritual and emotional strongholds like fear, shame, pride, insecurity, and control. When someone experiences rejection repeatedly, or even just severely once, they begin to live from it, not just through it. It becomes their lens.

The enemy knows this. Satan himself was the first being to be rejected from Heaven—cast out for rebellion. And ever since, he has worked to make people feel rejected by God, others, and even themselves.

The Difference Between Actual and Perceived Rejection

Not every feeling of rejection comes from real rejection. Sometimes what we perceive as rejection is actually:

- A miscommunication
- A moment of silence or absence
- A correction or boundary
- A difference in love languages or personality

But if your heart is already wounded, even silence can feel like abandonment. A look can feel like judgment. A delayed text can feel like betrayal. That's why it's crucial to recognize when you're responding to rejection based on truth versus when you're responding through the filter of past pain.

Perceived rejection is often more dangerous than real rejection—because it's harder to confront. The person didn't actually reject you, but your wounded lens convinced you they did.

The Common Types of Rejection

Let's break down the different forms of rejection people encounter—so you can begin to identify your own story.

1. Parental Rejection

- This is the most foundational form of rejection.
- It can come through abandonment, abuse, emotional distance, harshness, favoritism, or absence.
- A parent who was present physically but absent emotionally can create the same damage as one who left.
- Children who grow up without affirmation from their father or nurturing from their mother often internalize the lie: "I am not worth loving."

2. Peer and Social Rejection

- Bullying, cliques, gossip, betrayal, exclusion.
- Many people experience deep wounds in school, sports, or friend groups.
- Social rejection often triggers deep identity confusion and the beginning of people-pleasing or isolation.

3. Romantic Rejection

- Rejection from dating relationships, breakups, divorce, or unrequited love.
- These wounds often create a sense of inadequacy and lead to cycles of emotional dependence, fear of abandonment, or emotional detachment.

- Sexual rejection within marriage can also be a deep pain point.

4. Spiritual and Church Rejection

- Being overlooked by leaders, mistreated by authority, or excluded from ministry opportunities.
- Rejection from church family often causes the deepest kind of mistrust and spiritual confusion.
- Many associate the voice of God with the voice of wounded leaders—and shut down spiritually as a result.

5. Self-Rejection

- The most dangerous form—when rejection turns inward.
- This leads to self-hatred, perfectionism, harsh self-criticism, shame, and even self-harm.
- People may try to "fix" themselves endlessly, believing they're broken beyond repair.

6. Generational Rejection

- Rejection can run in families—passed down like a spiritual inheritance.
- Parents who never felt loved or accepted often fail to give it to their children.
- This creates a cycle where each generation continues operating out of a wound that was never healed.

Biblical Examples of Rejection

Rejection is not just a modern experience—it's a repeated theme in the Bible. God does not hide the stories of those who were rejected. Instead, He redeems them.

Cain

Rejected by God for offering what God did not ask for, Cain's response to perceived rejection became murderous rage. Rejection unhealed becomes destruction.

Leah

Jacob's unloved wife, Leah lived her life trying to earn affection by bearing sons. Her rejection led to striving—until she shifted her focus to the Lord. "Now I will praise the Lord," she said (Gen. 29:35). Worship healed her identity.

Joseph

Sold by his own brothers, rejected by family, and falsely accused by Potiphar's wife—Joseph experienced betrayal at every level. Yet he refused to let rejection define him. He kept his heart right and his vision clear.

David

Overlooked by his father, left out by his brothers, hunted by his king—David endured constant rejection. But the wilderness became the womb of intimacy. His identity was rooted in God's anointing, not man's approval.

Jesus

No one was rejected like Jesus. "He was despised and rejected by men; a man of sorrows and acquainted with grief" (Isaiah 53:3). Rejected by family, scorned by religious leaders, betrayed by friends, and crucified by those He came to save—Jesus bore every form of rejection so that you could be fully accepted.

Rejection Wears Many Masks

Rejection doesn't always look like pain. Sometimes it looks like:

- Pride: "I don't need anyone. I'll prove myself."
- Control: "I'll never let anyone hurt me again."
- Perfectionism: "If I'm perfect, I won't be rejected."
- Passivity: "If I stay quiet, I won't be a target."
- Isolation: "If I'm alone, at least I'm safe."
- People-pleasing: "If I make everyone happy, they'll keep me."

All of these are false protections—survival strategies that keep you locked in fear and hidden from healing.

A World Full of Wounds

The world is full of people walking around with rejection wounds they've normalized. They call it personality. They call it "just how I am." But deep down, many feel:

- Out of place
- Overlooked
- On edge
- On the outside
- Never enough

But here's the truth: You were never meant to live from rejection.

The pain is real. The wounds are deep. But they do not have the final word. You were made for belonging. You were created for connection. You were chosen before the foundation of the world. Rejection may have touched your life—but it does not define your identity.

The first step to freedom is recognizing where rejection has planted itself. It doesn't matter whether it came through childhood, relationships, or spiritual leadership. What matters now is that God wants to heal it.

This book is not just about healing a wound—it's about restoring a name. You are not rejected. You are not overlooked. You are not disqualified. You are accepted in the Beloved. Let's go deeper.

Reflection Questions

1. When have you most felt unseen, unwanted, or misunderstood? How did that moment shape how you see yourself today?

2. What "face" of rejection (fear, perfectionism, withdrawal, people-pleasing, etc.) do you most recognize in your life?

3. Ask the Holy Spirit to show you one relationship or season where rejection became a filter instead of a moment. What does He reveal?

2

HOW REJECTION ENTERS THE SOUL

*R*ejection doesn't need an invitation—it only needs an opening. It doesn't always come through a dramatic moment of betrayal or abuse; often it enters quietly, through subtle experiences, unmet needs, or small wounds that seem insignificant at first. But over time, rejection embeds itself deep into the soul and begins shaping how we think, feel, and relate. Before long, rejection is no longer something that happened to us—it becomes something we live from.

In this chapter, we'll explore the primary access points the spirit of rejection uses to enter and take root. By uncovering where it entered, we can begin the process of healing what it damaged.

The Soul: The Battleground of Identity

Your soul—comprised of your mind, will, and emotions—is where the enemy works to twist truth, distort identity, and fracture connection. What enters your soul through pain or trauma, if not healed, will become the internal voice that shapes your decisions and relationships.

The enemy's goal is simple: use rejection to form strongholds of unworthiness so that you live from a wounded identity. But the Holy Spirit wants to go to the place where rejection entered—not just to manage symptoms, but to heal the root.

Access Point 1: Early Life Wounds

The earliest years of your life matter more than most people realize. You may not consciously remember everything, but your soul does. Children interpret the world emotionally before they interpret it logically. This means that what felt like abandonment or indifference—even if it wasn't intended—can still plant seeds of rejection.

Parental Absence or Emotional Neglect

When a child doesn't receive affirmation, affection, or nurturing, their soul begins to question their value. Even parents who provided physical needs but failed to connect emotionally can unintentionally communicate, "You are not worth being known."

- Was your parent present but emotionally distant?
- Were you constantly compared to a sibling?
- Did you feel ignored, dismissed, or only noticed when in trouble?

All of these leave cracks in the soul that rejection can exploit.

Abuse and Betrayal

Physical, sexual, emotional, or verbal abuse sends a clear and destructive message: You are not safe. You are not valued. You are only a target or tool. Abuse not only wounds the soul— it opens the door to rejection, fear, shame, and self-hatred. Even after the abuse ends, the spirit of rejection stays until it is evicted and healed.

Abandonment or Adoption

Children who grow up without one or both parents often feel a deep-rooted sense of abandonment. Even if raised in a loving environment later, the absence creates a void that says, "If they really loved me, they would've stayed." The enemy uses that moment to establish a core lie: "If I were worth loving, they wouldn't have left."

Access Point 2: Performance-Based Love and Conditional Acceptance

Many people grew up in environments where love was tied to behavior, success, or compliance. Love became a reward for good performance rather than a secure foundation.

- "You got an A? I'm proud of you."
- "Why can't you be more like your brother?"
- "If you behave, you'll make mommy happy."

These messages may sound harmless, but over time, they create a belief system: I must perform to be loved. When the performance stops, the person feels disposable or invisible. This leads to perfectionism, burnout, and anxiety—and opens the soul to the spirit of rejection when expectations are unmet or mistakes are made.

Access Point 3: Favoritism and Comparison

Few wounds cut as deeply as favoritism. Whether real or perceived, the message is the same: You're not the one they want. Siblings who are favored for their talent, personality, or obedience can unknowingly cause the others to feel displaced or unloved.

This plays out not just in homes, but in classrooms, churches, and teams. When one person is constantly highlighted or elevated, others can begin to internalize rejection—even if no one intended it.

Comparison becomes the measuring stick. And when you constantly measure yourself against others, you will never feel like enough. The soul becomes fixated on what it lacks, and rejection takes root in the perceived gap.

Access Point 4: Bullying and Peer Rejection

For many, the deepest rejection didn't come from parents—it came from peers. Being mocked, excluded, or betrayed by friends leaves the soul shattered and the mind confused. "Why don't they like me? What's wrong with me?" These questions fester into insecurities that follow people for life.

The spirit of rejection tells you to hide or become who others want—either way, you lose yourself. This is where many develop masks: the funny one, the tough one, the quiet one—each designed to survive rejection rather than heal it.

Access Point 5: Generational Rejection and Iniquity

Rejection often runs in family lines. When a father never

received affection from his own father, he may not know how to give it. When a mother grew up feeling inferior or unloved, she may unconsciously pass that burden on to her children.

This is generational iniquity—patterns of pain that pass through bloodlines until someone decides to break the cycle. Often, these patterns are spiritual, not just psychological. Spirits of rejection, abandonment, fear, or control can attach themselves to families until they are renounced, resisted, and replaced with truth.

Access Point 6: Traumatic Events and Life Disruptions

Sometimes rejection enters through trauma that's not relational but situational:

- Divorce
- Financial hardship
- Moving schools or neighborhoods
- Death of a parent or close loved one
- Sudden illness or disability

These moments can be disorienting, leaving children or adults with a sense of loss, instability, or rejection by life itself. The enemy uses trauma as an entry point, whispering lies in the midst of crisis: "You're not safe. You're forgotten. You're different." If not processed through the Spirit of Truth, these moments become strongholds.

How the Enemy Exploits Open Doors

The enemy is legalistic. He looks for open doors—unforgiveness, lies, trauma, generational sin—and uses them to stake a claim. When rejection enters, it brings with it a demonic network:

- Fear (fear of man, fear of abandonment)
- Shame (I'm not enough, I'm broken)
- Control (I have to protect myself)
- Rebellion (I'll never trust again)
- Isolation (I'll pull away so they can't hurt me)

The longer rejection remains unhealed, the more these companions build strongholds in the soul. What began as a wound becomes an identity.

Recognizing Your Entry Points

Ask yourself:

- Where did I first feel unwanted, invisible, or not enough?
- Did I feel secure and celebrated in my childhood, or compared and criticized?
- Were there traumatic moments I never processed with God?
- Are there family patterns of emotional neglect, criticism, or abandonment?

Identifying your entry points doesn't reopen the wound—it exposes where healing is needed. You don't have to relive your past to be healed from it—but you must let the Holy Spirit shine His light on it.

Jesus Wants to Enter Where Rejection Entered

Here's the beautiful truth: Jesus wants to enter the very

place where rejection first entered you. He doesn't avoid your wounds—He walks into them. He doesn't shame you for your past—He redeems it. The moment of deepest pain can become the doorway to your greatest healing.

He stands at the door and knocks—not just the door of your salvation, but the door of your soul. The parts that hide. The memories you avoid. The version of yourself that still acts like a rejected child. He says, "Let Me in there. I want to bring truth where lies have lived. I want to heal the moment rejection rewrote your story."

From Entry to Eviction

You may not have chosen when rejection entered—but you get to choose when it leaves. This chapter is about exposure. The next chapters are about eviction, healing, and freedom. You are not bound to your wounds. You are not sentenced to repeat patterns. You are not too far gone. You are loved. And love is coming for every place rejection took root. Let's keep going.

Reflection Questions

1. Think back to your earliest memory of not feeling "enough." What message did rejection whisper to you then?

2. How have words, silence, or comparison from others wounded your sense of belonging?

3. Invite Jesus into one of those memories. What does He want to show you about where He was in that moment?

THE SPIRIT BEHIND THE PAIN

*R*ejection is more than a painful memory. It's more than an emotional wound. It is often a spirit, and it doesn't work alone. One of the greatest strategies of the enemy is to convince people that their battles are purely emotional, circumstantial, or personality-based. But Scripture is clear:

"For we do not wrestle against flesh and blood, but against principalities, against powers, against the rulers of the darkness of this age, against spiritual hosts of wickedness in the heavenly places."
(Ephesians 6:12) NKJV

What we often call insecurity, withdrawal, rage, or perfectionism is often rooted in a deeper spiritual stronghold. And one of the most common strongholds believers face—yet often misdiagnose—is the spirit of rejection.

This spirit doesn't just visit once. It builds a home. It crafts a language. It weaves lies into a person's identity. It's subtle, crafty, and persistent. But it is not unbreakable. And Jesus came to destroy its work.

The Spirit of Rejection Is Real

Let's be clear: not every person who struggles with rejection is demonized. Many rejection wounds are emotional in nature and can be healed through love, counseling, discipleship, and inner healing.

But in many cases—especially where rejection is chronic, irrational, or paralyzing—there is a demonic spirit at work behind the scenes. And until that spirit is discerned, renounced, and cast out, the cycle will repeat. Here's how the spirit of rejection operates:

- It enters through trauma, sin, abuse, or generational iniquity.
- It partners with lies to form a false identity.
- It manifests through emotions, behaviors, and relationships.
- It blocks the flow of God's love and distorts how you receive correction, affection, and authority.
- It isolates, torments, and ultimately attempts to destroy.

Rejection Doesn't Work Alone

The spirit of rejection rarely shows up alone. It often works in partnership with a demonic network designed to keep you trapped in cycles of defeat. Here are the most common spirits that run with rejection:

1. Fear

- Fear of man, fear of failure, fear of abandonment, fear of being alone.

- You become afraid to open up, afraid to try, afraid to be fully seen.
- Fear becomes a prison guard that keeps you from risking connection.

2. Insecurity

- Deep inner uncertainty about your worth, calling, or identity.
- Constant second-guessing, needing reassurance, craving validation.
- Insecurity is rejection's echo: "You're not enough. You never will be."

3. Shame

- Shame says, "Something is wrong with you."
- It keeps you hidden, apologizing for your existence, or performing to be accepted.
- Rejection opens the door; shame locks it from the inside.

4. Control

- A rejected soul often takes control to feel safe.
- Micromanaging, perfectionism, and hyper-independence become survival mechanisms.
- The lie: "If I control everything, I won't be rejected again."

5. Rebellion

- Some respond to rejection not with fear, but with defiance.

- "If they don't love me, I'll hurt them before they hurt me."
- This produces cycles of sabotage, broken relationships, and spiritual resistance to authority.

6. Pride

- Pride is often a mask for pain.
- It says, "I don't need anyone," but the truth is, "I'm afraid no one wants me."
- Rejected people sometimes build a false identity of superiority to avoid vulnerability.

7. Self-Hatred

- When rejection turns inward, it becomes self-hatred.
- You become your own worst critic.
- In extreme cases, this leads to self-harm, addiction, or suicidal thoughts.

The Orphan Spirit: Rejection's Deeper Agenda

Underneath the spirit of rejection is a deeper stronghold known as the orphan spirit. This spirit convinces people they are fatherless, unloved, unprotected, and on their own. Even believers can carry this mentality:

- Striving to earn what God freely gives.
- Competing with others for approval.
- Withdrawing when corrected.
- Feeling like a spiritual outsider, even in the family of God.

The orphan spirit blinds people to their true identity. It

robs them of rest. It makes sons live like slaves and daughters act like beggars. And worst of all, it makes people relate to God through fear rather than love.

But Romans 8:15 declares, "You did not receive the spirit of slavery to fall back into fear, but you have received the Spirit of adoption as sons, by whom we cry, 'Abba! Father!'" The Holy Spirit confronts the orphan spirit by revealing the Father's heart. Deliverance from rejection must be followed by a deep revelation of sonship.

How the Spirit of Rejection Operates

Let's take a look at some common ways this spirit manifests. These are signs that rejection may not just be emotional, but spiritual:

- You always assume people are mad at you.
- You misread silence or distance as personal offense.
- You feel invisible in rooms—even when people care.
- You feel a need to earn everything, even grace.
- You fear being corrected, exposed, or left out.
- You feel rejected even when no one has said anything.
- You sabotage relationships before they can reject you.
- You can't receive love without suspicion.

If you see yourself in these patterns, you are not crazy or weak. You're under attack. And now it's time to fight.

Jesus Came to Break This Spirit

Jesus didn't just die to forgive your sin. He died to break

every yoke, heal every wound, and drive out every demonic tormentor. The cross didn't just pay the price for Heaven—it crushed the authority of hell over your life.

> *"For this purpose the Son of God was manifested, that He might destroy the works of the devil." (1 John 3:8) NKJV*

And one of those works is rejection.

Jesus, who was perfectly loved by the Father, allowed Himself to be rejected by man so you could be accepted by God. His friends ran. His people mocked. His own creation crucified Him. And on the cross, He cried out, "My God, My God, why have You forsaken Me?"—not because the Father had abandoned Him, but because He took on the full weight of our separation so we could be brought back in.

You will never have to live rejected again. Because of Jesus, you are accepted, secure, and sealed in love.

Discerning the Spirit of Rejection

Here's how you begin the process of discerning whether the spirit of rejection is operating in your life:

- Ask the Holy Spirit: "When did rejection first enter?"
- Pay attention to patterns: Is there a consistent theme of rejection in relationships, jobs, or ministry?
- Notice your self-talk: Are you quick to assume you're being left out, judged, or unloved?
- Check your triggers: What moments make you spiral—silence, correction, exclusion?

Discernment is the beginning of deliverance.

Deliverance Is Real—and It's for You

There is no shame in needing deliverance. Jesus cast out demons not to shame people, but to set them free. And the spirit of rejection can be driven out—completely.

Later in this book, we'll walk through prayers of renunciation, deliverance, and identity declaration. But for now, recognize this: You don't have to manage rejection. You can be free from it.

The Holy Spirit is shining light into the dark corners where rejection has lived too long. And it's not to expose you for harm—but to expose the spirit so you can be healed.

Healing and Authority Go Hand in Hand

You don't just need comfort—you need authority. Deliverance and healing work together.

- Healing closes the wound.
- Deliverance breaks the agreement.
- Sonship restores your identity.

You're not just kicking out a spirit—you're reclaiming your name.

You're not rejected.
You're not forgotten.
You're not invisible.
You're not defective.
You are accepted. And that truth has the power to drive out every lie. Let's keep going.

Reflection Questions

1. What fruit has rejection produced in your life — fear, control, isolation, or striving?

2. When you feel rejected, what voice usually gets louder — the voice of love or the voice of accusation?

3. Ask the Holy Spirit to reveal where you've agreed with rejection's identity ("I'm not wanted," "I don't belong"). How can you renounce that agreement today?

4

THE SYMPTOMS OF A REJECTED LIFE

*R*ejection is rarely silent forever. Left unhealed, it eventually finds a voice—through your behavior, your emotions, and your relationships. Like an infection that spreads beneath the skin, the spirit of rejection creates symptoms that affect every area of life. It doesn't just make people feel unloved—it makes them live like they're unlovable.

Most people don't walk around saying, "I struggle with rejection." They say things like:

- "I feel like I don't belong."
- "I can't stop comparing myself to others."
- "I shut down when people correct me."
- "I try so hard and still feel invisible."
- "I'm terrified people will walk away."

These statements are not personality quirks—they are the fruit of an unhealed root.

This chapter will help you identify the symptoms of a

rejected life, not to shame you, but to awaken you. Awareness precedes healing. Once you recognize how rejection has affected your life, you can begin the process of replacing the lies with truth and the torment with peace.

1. Emotional Instability and Overreaction

People carrying rejection wounds often live on an emotional rollercoaster. One moment they're fine—the next, a small trigger sends them spiraling into insecurity, fear, or isolation.

- A leader walks past without saying hi → you assume you're being punished.
- A spouse forgets to text back → you feel abandoned.
- A friend chooses someone else → you assume they're tired of you.

These reactions are often disproportionate to the situation because they're not reacting to the present moment—they're reacting to past pain. When your soul hasn't been healed, every new disappointment feels like confirmation of an old lie.

2. Identity Confusion and Lack of Confidence

Rejection erodes identity. It makes you question who you are and where you fit. It tells you you're "too much" or "not enough"—sometimes both at once. It creates a fractured self-image that is constantly shaped by the opinions of others. You may find yourself:

- Constantly second-guessing your words and decisions.
- Needing others to affirm your ideas before you act.

- Shifting your personality depending on who you're with.
- Feeling like an imposter—even when you're qualified.

Instead of standing in God-given confidence, a rejected person waits for permission to be themselves.

3. Perfectionism and Performance

When love feels conditional, performance becomes survival. Many people who carry rejection are high achievers—not because they're confident, but because they're terrified of being overlooked. They believe, "If I succeed, I'll be loved. If I fail, I'll be rejected." This shows up as:

- Obsessive attention to detail.
- Fear of making mistakes.
- Workaholism or spiritual striving.
- An inability to rest without guilt.

Even ministry can become performance. Preaching, leading, and serving shift from joy to burden. You begin to work for God's love instead of from it.

4. Fear of Man and Social Anxiety

One of the clearest signs of rejection is living under the fear of people's opinions. You avoid confrontation, constantly read body language, or replay conversations in your head, wondering if you said something wrong. This fear produces:

- Anxiety in groups or leadership settings.
- Paralysis when making decisions.

- Exhaustion from trying to please everyone.
- A fear of being misunderstood, corrected, or disliked.

When rejection rules, man's opinion becomes louder than God's voice. You live for applause, avoid offense at all costs, and walk on eggshells in every relationship.

5. Self-Hatred and Internal Accusation

When rejection goes unchecked, it turns inward. The voice of rejection becomes your own voice, repeating phrases like:

- "I'm so stupid."
- "No one would choose me."
- "I'm always the problem."
- "I don't even like myself."

This internal critic feeds shame, depression, and hopelessness. It drives people to isolate, self-sabotage, or engage in destructive behaviors just to numb the pain. Some people turn to addiction, others to fantasy, others to toxic relationships—just to feel wanted for a moment.

Self-rejection is perhaps the most dangerous form, because it convinces you that healing is for everyone but you.

6. Isolation and Withdrawal

Many people assume that rejected individuals are clingy or needy—but often, they're guarded and distant. To avoid being hurt again, they keep everyone at arm's length.

- They struggle to let people get close.

- They smile on the outside but never open up.
- They withdraw when things get emotional.
- They self-protect through silence, busyness, or deflection.

Isolation may feel safe, but it's not healing. It's a prison built out of fear. And the longer you stay in it, the harder it becomes to remember what love feels like.

7. Relational Dysfunction and Sabotage

Rejection causes people to either cling too tightly or push people away. Both are rooted in fear.

- You expect people to leave, so you act distant to protect yourself.
- You fear abandonment, so you become overly dependent or controlling.
- You interpret healthy correction as personal attack.
- You sabotage good relationships before they can reject you.

This creates instability in marriage, friendships, church community, and even how people relate to God. You're always waiting for someone to leave, disappoint, or disapprove—and rejection becomes a self-fulfilling prophecy.

8. Victim Mentality and Powerlessness

A rejected life often leads to a victim mindset. You stop believing you have any power to change your story. You become defined by what happened to you rather than what Christ did for you. Victim mentality sounds like:

- "No one ever chooses me."
- "I always get left behind."
- "Things never work out for me."
- "It's just my personality—I've always been this way."

This mindset feeds depression, bitterness, jealousy, and apathy. It blocks faith, short-circuits hope, and paralyzes action. You live in survival mode—never expecting breakthrough. But you were not born to be a victim. You are more than a conqueror.

9. Resistance to Authority and Correction

Another major symptom is difficulty receiving correction without feeling crushed, attacked, or abandoned. For someone with rejection wounds, discipline feels like punishment. Accountability feels like betrayal.

- You feel misunderstood whenever someone brings a challenge.
- You avoid spiritual leadership out of fear of being "controlled."
- You either rebel—or shut down and internalize everything.

Rejection makes you interpret love through fear. But sonship interprets correction as care. Until rejection is healed, leadership will feel threatening instead of protective.

10. False Identities and Spiritual Mask-Wearing

In an effort to avoid future rejection, people begin to wear masks:

- The Funny One (hide pain with humor)
- The Strong One (never show weakness)
- The Spiritual One (hide behind performance or gifting)
- The Quiet One (never speak to avoid being wrong)
- The Successful One (win approval through results)

None of these are evil in themselves—but when used to protect instead of express, they become prisons. You weren't created to perform or pose. You were created to reflect the Father's image.

What These Symptoms Reveal

These symptoms are not random—they reveal where rejection has rooted itself in the soul. They are invitations to investigate, not reasons to condemn.

Think of these symptoms like a spiritual dashboard. When a light comes on in your car, you don't smash the light—you check the engine. In the same way, when fear, shame, insecurity, or withdrawal flare up, it's not a sign to hate yourself—it's a sign to invite the Holy Spirit into the root.

Healing Begins with Recognition

If you see yourself in these descriptions, don't run from it. Don't excuse it. Don't bury it under busyness, ministry, or numbness. Instead, say: "Holy Spirit, show me where this began. Help me see the lie I've been living under. I want truth to take root where rejection once ruled."

God doesn't expose to embarrass—He exposes to heal. Every symptom is a signal that love wants to go deeper.

You Don't Have to Live This Way Anymore

You were not made to walk on eggshells in your own life. You don't have to fight for visibility, approval, or acceptance. You don't have to prove your worth or guard your heart 24/7.

Jesus sees every symptom, and He understands every root. And He says, "I want to make you whole." This is not the end of your story—it's the beginning of your healing.

Reflection Questions

1. Which symptoms of rejection do you see recurring in your emotions or relationships?

2. What situations still trigger shame or the fear of being left out?

3. What would it look like to respond to rejection with truth instead of reaction?

5

THE APPROVAL TRAP — INSECURITY, PERFORMANCE, AND THE IDOL OF AFFIRMATION

*O*ne of the most deceptive fruits of rejection is the compulsion to perform for love. When someone doesn't know they're unconditionally loved, they begin trying to earn what should be freely received. They move from being to doing—from rest to striving. And behind all that effort is a question they don't know how to ask out loud: "Am I enough for you to stay?"

Rejection creates a hunger for affirmation, but not in a healthy way. It doesn't just desire encouragement—it needs it to survive. This creates a deadly trap: a cycle of insecurity, performance, and approval addiction. It's exhausting, toxic to relationships, and dangerous to your soul.

In this chapter, we'll expose the trap, identify how it affects you, and begin the journey toward freedom—a freedom rooted in the unwavering, unchanging, unearned approval of your Father in Heaven.

Insecurity: The Root That Fuels Performance

Insecurity is the inner doubt that says, "I don't know if I'm enough." When rejection has taken root in someone's soul, their confidence is no longer built on identity—it's built on performance and perception.

You can be talented, gifted, and called—but if insecurity is your root, you'll always feel like you're one misstep away from losing your place. Signs of insecurity rooted in rejection:

- Needing frequent affirmation to feel stable
- Being crushed by even gentle correction
- Constant comparison with others
- Anxiety in leadership or visibility
- Feeling like an imposter even when qualified

Insecurity doesn't mean you lack talent—it means you lack truth about who you are.

The Mask of Performance

Performance says, "If I do everything right, maybe I'll finally be loved."

When rejection teaches you that your value is tied to achievement, your life becomes a stage. You begin living for applause instead of alignment, acting out roles that win approval but betray your authentic self. This performance mindset shows up in:

- Ministry: Doing things for God to be seen by man
- Marriage: Trying to earn love by fixing, doing, or overachieving
- Parenting: Demanding perfection from your kids so you feel secure

- Church: Leading or serving out of fear of being forgotten

Eventually, performance leads to burnout. Because no matter how much you do—it never feels like enough.

The Idol of Affirmation

Affirmation is not wrong—it's a gift. But when it becomes a need, it becomes a god. Many believers unknowingly serve the idol of affirmation. They don't feel secure until someone says, "I'm proud of you," "You crushed it," or "We need you." But when affirmation becomes your fuel, you'll:

- Crave visibility more than intimacy
- Interpret silence as rejection
- Fear being overlooked more than being disobedient
- Do things just to be seen, even if God never asked you to

Affirmation is a gift from people—but it must never become your god. When it does, the opinions of man grow louder than the voice of God.

The Cycle: Insecurity → Performance → Approval Addiction

Here's how the cycle works:

1. Insecurity whispers: "You're not enough."
2. Performance responds: "Then I'll prove my worth."
3. Approval arrives: "They clapped. I'm safe... for now."
4. Insecurity returns: "What if next time they don't?"
5. The cycle repeats.

Even when affirmation comes, it's never enough to satisfy the soul—because the issue isn't your performance, it's your foundation.

You can't break this cycle by doing more. You break it by receiving the love you never had to earn.

Biblical Examples of the Trap

King Saul

Saul was anointed, chosen, and empowered by God—but he was deeply insecure. When the people praised David more than him, Saul spiraled into jealousy and fear (1 Sam. 18:7-9). He lived for the approval of man and ultimately lost the presence of God.

The Older Brother (Luke 15)

While the younger brother rebelled, the older brother performed. He stayed home, worked hard, followed the rules—but still didn't feel loved. He said to his father, "All these years I've served you, and you never gave me even a goat..." (Luke 15:29). His performance didn't lead to intimacy—it led to resentment.

Martha

Martha wasn't doing anything wrong—she was serving. But when Jesus came to visit, she missed the moment of connection because she was busy performing. She said, "Don't you care that I'm doing all the work?" (Luke 10:40). Rejection turns service into striving. But Jesus invites us to sit, not just serve.

What It Feels Like to Live in the Trap

You may be stuck in this trap if:

- You're only as happy as your last compliment.
- You fear losing roles or titles more than losing your soul.
- You find your value in results, not relationships.
- You can't say no because you fear disappointing others.
- You're never satisfied—even when you succeed.

This is slavery. It's not Kingdom. It's not freedom. And Jesus came to break it.

The Father's Approval Came First

When Jesus was baptized, He hadn't yet healed the sick, raised the dead, or preached the Sermon on the Mount. But the heavens opened, and the Father said:

"This is My beloved Son, in whom I am well pleased" (Matthew 3:17) NKJV

The Father's voice declared:

- Beloved — You are deeply loved.
- Son — You are part of My family.
- Well pleased — I delight in you before you do anything.

That is the foundation of your identity. Not performance. Not perfection. Not people. Just sonship.

From Striving to Sonship

To break the trap of approval, you must shift from living for love to living from love. This means:

- Repenting of the idol of affirmation
- Renouncing the lie that your worth is earned
- Receiving the Father's delight as your foundation
- Resting in being rather than doing

You are not what you do. You are who He says you are.

How to Break the Cycle

1. Name the Lies

Ask the Holy Spirit: "What lie did I believe that made me need to perform for love?" Write it down. Bring it into the light.

2. Renounce the Agreement

Say aloud: "I break agreement with the lie that I have to earn love. I renounce the idol of affirmation and the fear of being overlooked."

3. Declare Your Identity

Begin declaring daily:

"I am God's beloved child. I am already approved. I don't need to perform—I just need to abide. I rest in His delight."

4. Practice Obedience Without Applause

Do something only God sees. Say no when you would've

said yes out of fear. Worship when no one's watching. These are acts of warfare against approval addiction.

You Are Already Approved

You don't need another follower, another title, another breakthrough to be worthy of love. You are already loved—completely, unconditionally, eternally. The Father's voice is still speaking over you:

"You are My beloved. I am pleased with you."

Not because of what you've done. Not because of who you've impressed. But because you belong to Him. It's time to lay down the mask, the hustle, the stage—and return to the quiet place where you hear the only voice that matters.

Reflection Questions

1. In what ways have you sought approval or validation more than love and connection?

2. How does your need to "do" for God differ from simply being loved by Him?

3. What would change in your life if you no longer had to earn affirmation?

6

JESUS AND THE WOUND OF REJECTION

*J*esus, the Son of God, the Word made flesh, the only perfect person to ever live—was rejected. Not because He was flawed, but because He was the only one who could take on our flaws. And in the greatest act of love the world has ever seen, He absorbed every form of rejection so that we could be restored to love.

This is not just a theological truth—it is the foundation of your healing. Jesus didn't just die for you. He died as you. He stood in your place. He took the weight of sin, shame, abandonment, and rejection—so that you could take His place in the arms of the Father.

To heal from rejection, we must see Jesus rightly—not just as the Savior of our sin, but as the One who took the blow of every emotional and spiritual wound we carry. Every place where you've felt cast aside, unwanted, or alone—He already carried it.

Despised and Rejected by Men

"He is despised and rejected by men,
A Man of sorrows and acquainted with grief." (Isaiah 53:3) NKJV

Jesus knows the pain of rejection—personally. He was:

- Rejected by His hometown (Luke 4:28–30)
- Misunderstood by His family (Mark 3:21)
- Betrayed by a close friend (Luke 22:48)
- Denied by His closest disciple (Luke 22:61)
- Mocked by religious leaders (Mark 15:31)
- Abandoned by the crowds who once shouted His name (Mark 15:13)
- Crucified outside the city gate, as if to say: "You don't belong here." (Hebrews 13:12)

Even on the cross, His final cry reflected the depth of our separation:

"My God, My God, why have You forsaken Me?" (Matthew
27:46) NKJV

Though Jesus was never truly forsaken by the Father, in that moment, He bore the weight of humanity's exile—our rejection —so we would never be forsaken again.

He Took Our Place

Rejection isn't just a feeling—it's a separation. And Jesus came to bridge the divide.

At the cross, He didn't just deal with your sin. He dealt with your sorrow. Your sense of being cast off. Your need to prove yourself. Your fear of being unworthy. He didn't just forgive you —He carried what crushed you. Isaiah 53:4–5 says:

"Surely He has borne our griefs and carried our sorrows... He was pierced for our transgressions, crushed for our iniquities; the punishment that brought us peace was upon Him, and by His wounds we are healed." NIV

Let that sink in: He carried what you were never meant to carry. He didn't just die for your disobedience. He died for your brokenness. For your story. For the trauma you've managed, the lies you've believed, and the distance you've felt between yourself and love.

The Lamb Was Slain Outside the Camp

Hebrews 13:12–13 says:

"Jesus also suffered outside the city gate to make the people holy through His own blood. Let us, then, go to Him outside the camp, bearing the disgrace He bore." NIV

Why was He crucified outside the city? Because rejection took place outside the camp.

In Jewish culture, the rejected were cast outside: lepers, outcasts, criminals. Jesus identified with the outcast so completely that He allowed Himself to be pushed outside—so He could bring the outsider back in.

That's where He meets us—outside the religious systems, outside the performance trap, outside the walls we hide behind. He meets us in our disgrace and trades it for grace.

Accepted in the Beloved

Ephesians 1:6 says we are "accepted in the Beloved." That

word accepted means highly favored, fully received, and permanently welcomed. You don't have to fight for acceptance anymore. You don't have to audition for love. Jesus earned it for you. Because Jesus was rejected, you are:

- Accepted by the Father
- Welcomed into the family
- Affirmed without performance
- Loved without condition

The same voice that spoke over Jesus—"This is My beloved Son, in whom I am well pleased"—now echoes over you. Not because you earned it. But because you're in Him.

The Rejected One Became the Cornerstone

Psalm 118:22 declares:

"The stone the builders rejected has become the cornerstone." ESV

Rejection didn't disqualify Jesus—it positioned Him. In fact, it fulfilled prophecy. What man rejected, God exalted. What people cast aside, Heaven crowned. And that's what He'll do with your life too.

You may feel overlooked, unwanted, or disqualified. But in God's hands, rejection becomes redirection. He takes what others discard and makes it the foundation of something glorious. The cross is proof: What the world rejects, God redeems.

The Healing Power of His Rejection

When you bring your rejection to Jesus, you don't just get sympathy—you get substitution. He says:

- "I already carried that."
- "I already felt that."
- "I already paid for that."

When you feel abandoned—He knows what that feels like. When you feel overlooked—He's been there. When you feel unloved—He's still hanging on a cross, arms wide, saying, "This is love."

Your rejection is not too much for Him. He doesn't flinch at your pain. He moves toward it. And in that sacred exchange, your rejection is nailed to His cross—and His acceptance is placed on you like a royal robe.

What This Means for You

- You are no longer an outsider. You've been brought near by the blood of Christ (Eph. 2:13).
- You are not disqualified. You are chosen, holy, and dearly loved (Col. 3:12).
- You are not second-best. You are a royal priesthood, a treasured possession (1 Pet. 2:9).
- You are not invisible. Your name is written on His heart and engraved on His hands (Isa. 49:16).

Jesus didn't come just to get you into Heaven. He came to get Heaven into you. And that begins by healing the places where you've been cut off from love.

Healing Begins at the Cross

If you want to break free from rejection, you must come to the place where it was crucified. The cross is not just a symbol of salvation—it's the place where rejection lost its power.

The same blood that forgives your sin also heals your wounds. And today, that blood is still speaking—still cleansing, restoring, and reconciling. You don't have to carry rejection one more day. Jesus already did. Bring it to Him.

A Prayer for Healing

Jesus, You were despised and rejected so that I could be accepted. I bring You every moment I've felt unwanted, unseen, or unloved. I lay down the need to earn acceptance. I break agreement with every lie that says I'm not enough. I receive the truth: I am accepted in the Beloved. Because You were rejected, I am restored. Because You were cast out, I am brought in. Thank You, Jesus. Heal me where I've been wounded. Restore what rejection has stolen. Amen.

Reflection Questions

1. How does knowing that Jesus was rejected for you change how you see your own wounds?

2. Which part of His suffering—betrayal, abandonment, false accusation—feels most relatable to you?

3. What does His acceptance of you at the Cross reveal about your true worth?

7

REJECTION FILTERS — HOW IT DISTORTS RELATIONSHIPS, CORRECTION, AND CONNECTION

*W*hen rejection enters the soul, it doesn't just cause pain—it changes perception. It creates a filter, a lens that reshapes how you interpret the world around you. Even when people aren't rejecting you, it can feel like they are. What someone else sees as a neutral moment, you experience as abandonment. What they meant as correction, you feel as rejection. What they meant as rest, you feel as silence or being forgotten.

Rejection becomes a filter—and until it's removed, it keeps twisting the truth, sabotaging relationships, and blocking the very love you were created to receive.

This chapter will help you recognize that filter and learn how to replace it with the clarity, safety, and confidence that comes from true sonship.

Rejection Creates a False Narrative

When someone walks through years of rejection—real or

perceived—their heart becomes conditioned to expect pain. That expectation begins writing a false story in real time. Here's how it plays out:

- A leader corrects you → "They don't value me."
- A spouse is quiet → "They're losing interest."
- A friend forgets to text → "I'm always forgotten."
- Someone gives someone else attention → "I'm replaceable."

These assumptions aren't based on facts. They're based on filters. Your rejection filter tells you what's happening before you even ask or listen. It defines reality for you. And it lies.

When You See Through a Filter, You Can't See the Truth

Rejection filters twist everything:

- Authority becomes threat: You see leaders as people who will hurt, abandon, or silence you—not as those called to protect, guide, and cover you.
- Correction becomes rejection: You hear loving feedback as personal failure or condemnation.
- Silence becomes distance: A quiet moment from a friend or pastor feels like emotional disconnection or judgment.
- Disagreement becomes disapproval: If someone sees things differently, it feels like they're withdrawing their love.
- Absence becomes abandonment: Even when people are busy or overwhelmed, you perceive their absence as a decision to discard you.

This is how rejection breeds insecurity, fear of man, anxiety, and relational sabotage.

How Rejection Interprets Different Relationships

Let's break down how rejection can distort how we view key people in our lives:

1. Leaders and Authority Figures

- You assume they're always evaluating you.
- You fear being disciplined, challenged, or left out.
- You struggle to trust their intentions or motives.
- When they lead from love, you hear control.
- When they challenge you, you hear abandonment.

2. Spouses and Romantic Relationships

- You crave constant reassurance, or you shut down emotionally.
- You interpret absence or quietness as rejection.
- You read too much into body language, silence, or tone.
- You compare yourself to others they interact with.
- You assume they'll eventually grow tired of you or walk away.

3. Friends and Peers

- You expect to be excluded or overlooked.
- You feel on the outside, even when you're included.
- You overanalyze group dynamics and conversations.
- You feel hurt when people don't reach out "enough."

- You assume everyone else has deeper bonds than you do.

4. Children or Those You Lead

- You project your wounds onto them.
- You over-correct to control outcomes and avoid pain.
- You become overly protective or emotionally disconnected.
- You misread their behavior as rejection or dishonor.
- You unintentionally parent or lead through fear.

5. God

- You feel like you're never doing enough to please Him.
- You struggle to trust His silence or discipline.
- You wonder if He's disappointed in you more than delighted.
- You compare your journey to others and feel spiritually "less than."
- You try to earn closeness instead of receiving it.

When rejection is your lens, no one feels safe. Even God's voice can feel distant, uncertain, or condemning.

Examples of Filtered Thinking

Rejection filters sound like this:

- "They didn't say hi—must be mad at me."
- "They didn't ask me to join—guess I'm not wanted."
- "They looked upset—what did I do wrong?"
- "They haven't checked in—I knew they didn't care."

- "They corrected me—I'm probably being pushed out."

None of these conclusions are necessarily true. But when your soul is trained to expect rejection, it doesn't need proof—it just needs a whisper. This is why the enemy doesn't need to launch a full assault—he just needs to suggest something. Your filter does the rest.

Where the Filter Comes From

These filters often come from:

- Childhood pain: You felt unwanted or invisible growing up.
- Relational trauma: Betrayals, heartbreak, or church wounds.
- Disciplinary abuse: Harsh correction that crushed your heart.
- Unmet emotional needs: Lack of affection, attention, or affirmation.
- Legalism or religion: Being taught that love must be earned.

What begins as protection becomes prison. The filter is not keeping you safe—it's keeping you stuck.

How the Filter Sabotages Connection

The rejection filter causes you to:

- Withdraw before anyone has a chance to love you.
- Test people's loyalty with unhealthy expectations.

- Cling to people out of fear, then push them away in shame.
- Interpret every silence as a sign that you don't belong.
- Mislabel safe correction as spiritual abuse.
- Live on edge, walking in suspicion instead of trust.

It sabotages covenant. It prevents restoration. And it numbs your ability to recognize healthy love when it finally comes.

Sonship Heals Your Vision

When you receive the Spirit of adoption, your lens changes. You begin to interpret life through love, not fear.

"You did not receive the spirit of slavery to fall back into fear, but you received the Spirit of adoption by whom we cry, 'Abba! Father!'"
(Romans 8:15) ESV

The Spirit of adoption rewrites how you see:

- God's correction becomes love, not punishment.
- Leadership's boundaries become safety, not exclusion.
- Silence becomes invitation, not abandonment.
- Accountability becomes affirmation, not attack.

When you live as a son or daughter, you know you belong. You no longer demand perfection from others, because you've received perfect love from the Father.

How to Dismantle the Filter

1. Ask the Holy Spirit to Show You the Filter

Pray:

"Lord, where have I been seeing people through pain? What moment in my past taught me to expect rejection?"

He will reveal the memory or moment that created the lens.

2. Present Jesus in That Memory

Invite Him to speak truth into that place:

"Jesus, what do You want to say to me about that moment?"

Truth displaces the lie and begins to heal the perception.

3. Renounce the Filter

Say aloud:

"I break agreement with the lie that I will always be rejected, misunderstood, or left out. I renounce the rejection filter and receive the mind of Christ."

4. Practice Interpreting Through Sonship

When someone is distant, don't assume rejection—assume they are human. When corrected, remind yourself: "I am still loved." When left out, tell yourself: "My worth hasn't changed." This is spiritual warfare at the relational level. And you win by choosing trust over fear.

You Were Meant to See Clearly

God wants to heal how you see. He wants to give you pure

eyes—unfiltered by pain, undistorted by fear, and unclouded by the past. You will not always feel misunderstood. You will not always interpret love as loss. You will not always need to defend yourself or overanalyze everything said—or unsaid. You are a son. You are a daughter. You are secure. Jesus didn't just come to fix your relationships—He came to heal your perspective.

It's time to put down the rejection lens and pick up the truth: You are fully accepted. You belong here. You are safe.

Reflection Questions

1. How might rejection be distorting how you interpret correction, love, or connection?

2. Who in your life do you struggle to receive from because of past hurt?

3. Ask Jesus to replace your rejection lens with His perspective. What do you see differently now?

PART II

THE HEALING JOURNEY TO ACCEPTANCE

8

EXPOSING THE LIES, RECEIVING THE TRUTH

*R*ejection doesn't just hurt—it lies. And if those lies aren't exposed, they become the foundation you live on. You may be saved, Spirit-filled, and outwardly functional, but inwardly tormented by thoughts that sound like your voice —but were never meant to be yours.

Rejection enters through wounds, but it survives through agreements. The moment you start believing the lie, you empower it to shape your identity. And until that lie is exposed and replaced, healing remains incomplete.

This chapter will help you locate the lies rejection taught you, recognize their fruit, and walk through the process of exchange—where Jesus reveals truth, restores your identity, and breaks the cycle for good.

The Lie Is the Real Stronghold

2 Corinthians 10:4–5 says:

"For the weapons of our warfare are not carnal but mighty in God for pulling down strongholds, casting down arguments and every high thing that exalts itself against the knowledge of God, bringing every thought into captivity to the obedience of Christ" NKJV

Strongholds aren't just demons—they are lies you believe to be true. A stronghold is a fortified thought pattern that resists the truth of God's Word and keeps you in bondage. And the enemy's favorite lies sound like this:

- "I'm not wanted."
- "I'll always be on the outside."
- "I'm too much."
- "I'm not enough."
- "They're just being nice—they don't really like me."
- "If they knew the real me, they'd leave."
- "I have to earn my place."
- "I'll never be like them."
- "I don't fit here."
- "I'm always overlooked."

Every one of these lies has a root. And behind that root is a moment, a wound, or a pattern where rejection first entered.

How Lies Are Formed

Lies are planted in moments of emotional intensity—especially when you're young or vulnerable. They're often unspoken but felt deeply. For example:

- A parent consistently criticizes you → You believe, "I can't do anything right."
- A friend betrays you → You believe, "I'm replaceable."

- A leader ignores your voice → You believe, "I'm not significant."
- A spouse withdraws emotionally → You believe, "I'm unlovable."

Once the lie is planted, you start collecting evidence to reinforce it. Every new disappointment confirms the old narrative. This creates a distorted "truth" that feels so real, you don't even question it anymore.

But God is not obligated to bless the false version of you. He only anoints the real you—the one created in His image and secured by His truth.

Truth Doesn't Just Inform—It Transforms

John 8:32 says,

> *"You will know the truth, and the truth will make you free."*
> *NASB1995*

Truth isn't just information. It's liberation. The Greek word for "know" in this verse implies intimate, experiential knowledge—not head-level facts, but heart-level revelation. It's the kind of knowing that breaks chains and restores identity. You don't just need to hear truth—you need to encounter it in the place where the lie first entered.

The Process: Presenting the Pain to Jesus

Here's the inner healing process we walk through when identifying and replacing lies. This is not a formula—it's a relational, Spirit-led encounter:

1. Identify the Lie

Ask the Holy Spirit:

> "What lie did I believe in that moment?"

Wait. Let the memory or phrase come. Don't rush it. Don't rationalize it. Just acknowledge it.

2. Invite Jesus into the Memory

Ask:

> "Jesus, where were You when this happened?"

Let Him reveal Himself in the memory. Many people are shocked by what they see—Jesus sitting beside them, weeping with them, shielding them, or speaking truth in the chaos.

3. Listen for His Truth

Ask:

> "Jesus, what do You want me to know about this moment?"

You might hear Him say:

- "You were never alone."
- "You didn't deserve that."
- "I've always wanted you."
- "They left, but I never did."
- "You are Mine."

Write down what He says. That truth becomes your new foundation.

4. Forgive and Release

Forgive the person who planted the wound—even if they never asked. Forgiveness doesn't excuse their behavior; it releases you from the hold it has on you. Forgive yourself if needed. Repent for believing the lie. Break agreement with it in Jesus' name.

Examples of the Exchange

Let's look at some common lies and the truths that dismantle them:

- Lie: "I'm unwanted."
- Truth: "I chose you before the foundation of the world." (Eph. 1:4)
- Lie: "I'm always overlooked."
- Truth: "The Father sees what is done in secret and rewards you." (Matt. 6:6)
- Lie: "I'm not enough."
- Truth: "My grace is sufficient for you." (2 Cor. 12:9)
- Lie: "I have to earn love."
- Truth: "You are saved by grace, not by works." (Eph. 2:8–9)
- Lie: "I don't belong."
- Truth: "You are no longer a stranger but a fellow citizen with the saints." (Eph. 2:19)
- Lie: "I'm on my own."
- Truth: "I will never leave you or forsake you." (Heb. 13:5)

The enemy uses the lie to control your behavior. God uses the truth to restore your identity.

From False Identity to True Sonship

Lies create false identities—counterfeit versions of yourself that you wear to survive:

- The Overachiever
- The Clown
- The Chameleon
- The Isolator
- The People-Pleaser
- The Critic

Each one is a strategy to avoid further rejection. But the longer you wear the false self, the harder it is to receive authentic love—because you start to believe your mask is your identity. But the Father didn't create the mask. He created you. The Spirit of Truth is not here to shame you. He's here to restore you.

You Were Not Created to Live in a Lie

The truth is:

- You are loved—without condition.
- You are seen—even in silence.
- You are wanted—without needing to prove it.
- You are accepted—in the Beloved.

And every time you receive that truth in the place where rejection lied to you, the root breaks. That's how healing happens—not by managing pain, but by meeting Jesus in the memory and letting His truth take over.

Practical Exercise: Walking Through the Exchange

Here's a moment-by-moment prayer model you can use on your own or with others:

1. Holy Spirit, what lie have I believed about myself (wait and listen)
2. When did I first believe that lie?
3. (allow Him to bring a memory or impression)
4. Jesus, where were You in that moment? What do You want to show me? (ask Him to reveal His truth in that place)
5. I choose to forgive the person involved, and I break agreement with the lie. (pray aloud)
6. I declare the truth: [insert what Jesus showed you].
7. (speak it over yourself)

Do this every time a trigger hits, a lie surfaces, or a memory reopens.

The Truth Will Set You Free

You don't need another sermon—you need an encounter. The Father's voice is louder than the lie, and His Word is stronger than the wound. And His Spirit is ready to walk you into truth that sets your soul free.

Let rejection be evicted. Let false identity be broken. Let the truth be your new foundation. You are not who rejection said you are. You are who the Father says you are.

Reflection Questions

1. What lie about yourself or God do you most struggle to stop believing?

2. When truth confronts that lie, how do you typically respond — resist, rationalize, or receive?

3. What does God's truth say about your identity in that area?

9

FORGIVENESS — THE KEY TO FREEDOM

There is no deep healing without deep forgiveness. You can identify every lie, confront every wound, and cast out every spirit—but if forgiveness is withheld, freedom will remain just out of reach.

Forgiveness is not a feeling. It is a decision—a divine act of obedience and trust that opens the door to healing, wholeness, and restoration. But for those who've experienced deep rejection, betrayal, or abandonment, forgiveness can feel impossible. It can feel like letting the offender off the hook. It can feel unsafe. But what if forgiveness isn't about excusing the wound? What if it's about exposing the chain?

Forgiveness doesn't say, "It didn't matter." Forgiveness says, "I refuse to be bound by what happened." And it is the key that unlocks your prison and releases the power of the cross into your past, your identity, and your future.

Unforgiveness and the Spirit of Rejection

One of the ways the spirit of rejection maintains its grip on a person's soul is through unforgiveness. Here's how the cycle works:

- You are rejected or abandoned.
- Pain turns into bitterness.
- Bitterness fuels inner vows and false beliefs.
- Unforgiveness creates a legal foothold for torment (Matthew 18).
- You live bound to the very people who hurt you.

Rejection attaches itself to pain, but unforgiveness keeps it alive. Every time you replay what they did. Every time you imagine confronting them. Every time you feel the sting when their name is mentioned. You're reinforcing the stronghold.

Jesus Takes Forgiveness Personally

In Matthew 6:14–15, Jesus said:

"If you forgive others their trespasses, your heavenly Father will also forgive you, but if you do not forgive others... neither will your Father forgive your trespasses." ESV

Forgiveness is not optional in the Kingdom. It's not for the emotionally mature. It's not for those who feel ready. It's for anyone who's been forgiven. The cross is not just where you were forgiven. It's where you lost the right to withhold forgiveness from anyone else. Jesus paid for their sin too.

Forgiveness and Emotional Justice

Let's be honest—sometimes we want justice more than healing. We want the person to feel what we felt. We want closure, apology, admission. But when you live demanding emotional justice, you become the jailer of your own soul. And the person who hurt you continues to hold power over you— not because they still have access to your life, but because you're still carrying them in your heart. Forgiveness is not a denial of justice. It's a transfer of justice—to God. Romans 12:19 says:

> *"Vengeance is Mine, says the Lord. I will repay." NKJV*

Forgiveness says, "God, You're the Judge. I release them from my judgment. I release myself from the pain."

Who Do You Need to Forgive?

You may need to forgive:

- A parent who abandoned, abused, or emotionally neglected you.
- A spiritual leader who shamed, silenced, or betrayed you.
- A spouse who broke covenant, withdrew emotionally, or used words as weapons.
- A friend who gossiped, rejected, or replaced you.
- A sibling who was favored over you.
- A boss or coworker who overlooked and undervalued you.
- A coach, mentor, or teacher who belittled you.
- Yourself—for agreeing with lies and sabotaging your life.
- God—not because He sinned, but because you blamed Him for your pain.

You may think, "I've already forgiven them." But if the

memory still triggers rage, sorrow, or defensiveness, there may still be unresolved pain. Forgiveness is not forgetting. It's remembering without bondage.

What Forgiveness Is and Is Not

Let's clear up some lies about forgiveness:

Forgiveness is NOT:

- Saying what they did was okay.
- Letting them back into your life unsafely.
- Trusting them again immediately.
- Feeling good about what happened.

Forgiveness IS:

- Releasing them from your judgment.
- Canceling the emotional debt they owe you.
- Inviting God into the place where the pain happened.
- Allowing Jesus to be the Healer and the Judge.

Forgiveness sets you free—not them.

Forgiving from the Heart

In Matthew 18:21–35, Jesus tells the story of the unforgiving servant—a man forgiven of an enormous debt who refused to forgive someone else a much smaller one. The result? He was handed over to torment until he forgave. Jesus ends the parable with these chilling words:

"So My heavenly Father also will do to each of you, if you do not forgive your brother from your heart." (Matthew 18:35) NKJV

Forgiveness from the heart doesn't mean emotional perfection. It means full surrender:

- "God, I choose to release them."
- "I cancel the emotional debt."
- "I release my right to revenge."
- "I bless them and ask You to restore me."

How to Walk Through Forgiveness

Here's a guided prayer process to walk through emotional and spiritual forgiveness:

1. Name the Person and the Pain

"Jesus, I bring [name] before You. They hurt me when they [describe it honestly]. That moment made me feel [rejected, abandoned, unworthy, invisible]."

2. Acknowledge the Emotional Cost

"That pain has cost me [connection, peace, joy, confidence, trust, identity]."

3. Release the Debt

"But today, I choose to forgive them. I cancel the debt they owe me. I release them from my judgment. I place this pain into Your hands."

4. Ask Jesus to Speak Truth

"Jesus, what do You want me to know about this moment? What is the truth You are giving me in exchange for the pain?" Wait. Listen. Write it down.

5. Bless and Break Agreement

"I bless [name] in Your name. I break agreement with bitterness, rejection, and revenge. I declare that I am not what they did—I am who You say I am."

What Happens After Forgiveness?

Forgiveness doesn't always lead to instant emotional relief —but it always opens the door to healing. After forgiveness, you may experience:

- Peace where anxiety lived
- Freedom where tension ruled
- Compassion where anger burned
- Clarity where confusion clouded
- Authority where torment had power

You are no longer tethered to their sin. You are free.

The Fruit of a Forgiving Heart

When forgiveness becomes your lifestyle, you'll find:

- You can confront without attacking.
- You can walk away without resentment.
- You can set boundaries without bitterness.
- You can be corrected without spiraling.
- You can lead and love from a healed heart.

Forgiveness doesn't make you weak—it makes you powerful. Because nothing has greater authority than a heart healed by love.

You Were Made for Freedom

The chains of rejection are rusted and ready to fall. But the key is still in your hand.

You don't need to wait for an apology.
You don't need to wait until it stops hurting.
You don't need to wait until they "get it."

You need to forgive. And when you do, the prison door opens—not just for them, but for you.

Reflection Questions

1. Who still comes to mind when you think of rejection's pain?

2. What emotions arise when you imagine forgiving them?

3. Ask Jesus to show you what freedom could look like on the other side of forgiveness.

10

RENOUNCING THE SPIRIT OF REJECTION

*H*ealing is powerful. Forgiveness is transformational. But deliverance is the final blow to the spirit of rejection. Many believers carry wounds that have been tended to, lies that have been exposed, and even hearts that have forgiven—but they still feel bound. They still struggle with irrational fear, constant insecurity, and invisible resistance that feels spiritual.

That's because rejection isn't just a wound or a lie—it's often a spirit. And it must be cast out. You can't counsel a demon. You can't comfort it, manage it, or reason with it. You must confront it. And then evict it in the name of Jesus.

This chapter is about breaking agreement with the spirit of rejection and all its companions—through repentance, renunciation, and declaration—so that your soul can be fully free to walk in sonship.

Deliverance Is Part of Your Inheritance

Jesus didn't just come to forgive sins—He came to destroy demonic strongholds. 1 John 3:8 says:

"The Son of God appeared for this purpose, to destroy the works of the devil." NASB1995

Luke 4:18 says:

"He has sent Me to proclaim liberty to the captives and the opening of the prison to those who are bound..." NKJV

Deliverance is not weird. It's not reserved for extreme cases. It's normal in the Kingdom. It's the children's bread. (Mark 7:27)

If rejection has rooted itself in your soul through trauma, unforgiveness, generational patterns, or deep emotional wounds—it may have become a demonic stronghold. That stronghold must be broken, and the spirit behind it cast out.

Recognizing When Deliverance Is Needed

You may need deliverance if:

- You've done inner healing but still feel heavy, tormented, or stuck.
- You've forgiven, but the emotional weight won't lift.
- You feel rage, jealousy, or fear rise up uncontrollably.
- You're filled with shame no matter how much truth you know.
- You feel an irrational fear of abandonment in safe relationships.
- You feel numb, unseen, or disconnected—even with people who love you.

These are not always just emotional responses—they are signs of spiritual bondage. Deliverance is not for the possessed—it's for the oppressed. And Jesus is ready to set you free.

The Power of Renunciation

Renunciation is a spiritual act where you:

- Break agreement with a lie or spirit.
- Cancel its legal right to remain.
- Declare the truth of God's Word over your life.

The enemy cannot stay where agreement has been broken. When you renounce a spirit, you remove its permission to operate in your life. Renunciation is not a ritual. It's a bold declaration of authority—rooted in Christ.

Common Spirits That Partner With Rejection

Rejection rarely works alone. When you break with rejection, you often need to renounce its whole network. These include:

- Fear (of man, abandonment, failure)
- Insecurity (self-doubt, inferiority)
- Shame (self-hatred, embarrassment)
- Control (manipulation, perfectionism)
- Pride (hiding, defensiveness)
- Rebellion (resistance to authority)
- Isolation (withdrawal, passivity)
- Depression (hopelessness, despair)
- Victimhood (entitlement, blame)
- Religious striving (earning love through works)

You don't need to fear these spirits. You have been given authority over them. Luke 10:19 says:

"I have given you authority... over all the power of the enemy, and nothing shall by any means harm you." NKJV

Preparing for Renunciation and Deliverance

Before we go into prayer, take a moment to:

1. Repent for partnering with these spirits.
2. Forgive anyone who opened the door to them.
3. Surrender any part of your identity that has been built on the lie of rejection.

Ask the Holy Spirit:

"Is there any part of me still tied to rejection, fear, or shame?"

Let Him show you. Don't rush. When ready, move into the declaration and prayer.

Prayer of Renunciation and Deliverance

In the name of Jesus Christ, I break every agreement I've made with the spirit of rejection. I renounce the lie that I am unwanted, unworthy, unloved, or unseen. I break every soul tie, inner vow, and generational curse tied to rejection. I renounce and command to leave: the spirit of fear, shame, insecurity, control, rebellion, pride, self-hatred, isolation, depression, striving, and victimhood.

You have no place in my life. I command every spirit that entered through rejection to go now—out of my soul, my mind, my emotions, and my body—in Jesus' name. Holy Spirit, fill every place that was emptied. I receive the Spirit of adoption. I receive perfect love that casts out fear. I receive the truth: I am accepted in the Beloved. I belong. I am wanted. I am chosen. I am loved.

I declare that my identity is not built on people's opinions, but on the Father's voice. Jesus, thank You for setting me free. I walk in freedom, healing, and authority—from this day forward. Amen.

What to Expect After Deliverance

After true deliverance, many people experience:

- A feeling of lightness or peace
- Physical release (tears, yawning, trembling, deep sighs)
- Mental clarity
- New confidence and joy
- Greater ability to receive love and give it without fear

Sometimes deliverance is immediate. Other times, it happens in layers. Don't judge the experience—celebrate the freedom. Stay in a posture of worship, gratitude, and Word-filled meditation. Continue declaring truth every day.

Sealing Your Freedom in Sonship

Deliverance is a beginning, not the end. You must now build your life on the truth you declared. Here's how:

- Spend time in the Word daily—especially Scriptures about identity.
- Surround yourself with spiritual family who will reinforce truth.
- Watch for old patterns—and replace them with new habits of grace.
- Keep short accounts—walk in ongoing forgiveness and humility.
- Speak life over yourself every day: "I am accepted. I am loved. I am safe."

The Spirit of adoption wants to fill the places rejection once occupied. Let Him. Talk to the Father like a child talks to a parent. Receive love without performing. Let sonship become your foundation.

You Are Free

- You don't belong to fear.
- You don't belong to shame.
- You don't belong to the opinions of others.
- You don't belong to rejection.
- You belong to the Father.

The chains are broken. The spirits have been evicted. And the voice of rejection has been silenced. Now it's time to live like a son.

Reflection Questions

1. What agreements or inner vows ("I'll never trust again," "I'll always be alone") have you made in pain?

2. What would it mean to break those vows and speak truth in their place?

3. Pray: "Holy Spirit, what lie do You want to silence in me today?" Write what He says.

11

HEALING SELF-REJECTION AND SHAME

The most dangerous voice of rejection is the one that sounds like your own. It begins when you stop blaming others and start blaming yourself. You internalize the pain. You wear the failure. You take responsibility not only for what happened—but for what it made you believe about you. And just like that, rejection isn't coming from the outside anymore. It's coming from within.

This is the pain of self-rejection—when the wound rejection caused becomes the lens through which you see yourself. Instead of healing, you start punishing yourself. You adopt shame as your identity. You stop hoping for love and start settling for silence. This chapter is about breaking that agreement.

- You're not unworthy.
- You're not a burden.
- You're not a mistake.

You are the beloved of God. And it's time to love the person He loves—you.

How Rejection Turns Inward

Every time someone else rejected you—if it wasn't healed—it invited you to start rejecting yourself.

- They said, "You're not enough" → You believed, "I'm a failure."
- They ignored you → You decided, "I must be invisible."
- They criticized you → You started repeating it to yourself.
- They left you → You concluded, "I must be the problem."

It starts subtly—small, toxic agreements:

- "Why do I always ruin things?"
- "I'm so stupid."
- "No one wants to deal with me."
- "I never do anything right."
- "It's probably my fault."

These inner statements are not humility—they are hatred in disguise. And they open the door to self-sabotage, shame, and emotional isolation.

The Fruit of Self-Rejection

If self-rejection has taken root, you'll see it in patterns like these:

1. Harsh Inner Critic

You talk to yourself in ways you'd never talk to others:

- "You're an idiot."
- "You always mess this up."
- "What's wrong with you?"

It's not correction—it's condemnation.

2. Perfectionism and Fear of Failure

You set impossible standards and beat yourself up for not meeting them. You associate failure with identity: "If I mess up, I am a mess."

3. Inability to Receive Love

When someone affirms you, your first thought is:

- "They don't mean it."
- "They don't know the real me."
- "They feel obligated."

You reject love as soon as it comes.

4. Constant Comparison

You see others as valuable, anointed, beautiful—but not yourself. You believe you're fundamentally flawed. You admire others while silently disqualifying yourself.

5. Self-Sabotage

You destroy opportunities, end relationships, and avoid risk —because deep down, you don't believe you deserve blessing or success.

6. Self-Harm or Destructive Behavior

In extreme cases, self-rejection leads to eating disorders, self-injury, addiction, or suicidal thoughts. These are not just psychological—they are spiritual cries: "Make the pain stop."

The Spirit of Shame

Self-rejection always partners with shame. If guilt says, "I did something wrong," Shame says, "Something is wrong with me."

Shame hides. It avoids eye contact. It stays silent in community. It keeps secrets. It covers itself with fig leaves—just like Adam and Eve did when they sinned. But Jesus came to undo shame.

"For the joy set before Him, He endured the cross, scorning its shame"
(Hebrews 12:2) NIV

He didn't just take your sin—He scorned your shame.

Jesus Doesn't Reject You—Even When You Do

"Whoever comes to Me, I will never cast out." (John 6:37) ESV

That includes you. Even when you've cast yourself aside, Jesus won't. Even when you speak against yourself, He still speaks truth. Even when you hide, He pursues. Even when you reject your reflection, He sees His image in you. Healing begins when you stop agreeing with your broken opinion—and start agreeing with the Father's voice.

Learning to Love Yourself in a Holy Way

Loving yourself is not narcissism. It's obedience. Jesus said:

"Love your neighbor as you love yourself." (Mark 12:31) NLT

If you hate yourself, you will inevitably hurt others. But when you love yourself as God does, you can love others from abundance, not emptiness. Here's what holy self-love looks like:

- Speaking truth over yourself—even when you feel weak.
- Receiving correction without self-condemnation.
- Allowing people to love you without suspicion.
- Treating your body, mind, and soul with honor.
- Refusing to agree with the enemy about your worth.

The Father's Voice Over You

If you've lived with self-rejection, it's time to hear what your Father actually says about you:

- "You are fearfully and wonderfully made." (Psalm 139:14)
- "You are My child, whom I love." (Romans 8:16)
- "You are a new creation in Christ." (2 Corinthians 5:17)
- "You are not condemned." (Romans 8:1)
- "You are accepted in the Beloved." (Ephesians 1:6)

You don't have to fight for love. You already have it. You

don't have to earn approval. You already carry it. You don't have to perform for belonging. You were born for it.

Steps to Heal Self-Rejection

1. Repent for Agreeing with Self-Hatred

Say:

"Father, forgive me for rejecting myself. I break agreement with every lie that says I'm unworthy, broken, or too much. I repent for speaking death over my own life. I receive Your truth."

2. Renounce the Spirit of Shame

Say:

"In Jesus' name, I renounce shame and self-hatred. I command every spirit of torment tied to rejection to leave. I receive the Spirit of adoption and the love of the Father."

3. Declare Your Identity Daily

Speak life over yourself:

- "I am chosen."
- "I am loved."
- "I am made in the image of God."
- "I am enough—not because I earned it, but because He said so."

4. Practice Self-Compassion

- Give yourself permission to heal slowly.

- Celebrate small wins.
- Let the Holy Spirit speak kindly to the places you once punished.

A Personal Declaration for Healing

Heavenly Father,
I receive Your love—
not just in theory, but for me.
I am not a mistake.
I am not too much.
I am not too broken.
I am exactly who You made me to be.
I choose to see myself the way You see me.
I love what You love—and that includes me.
I lay down the voice of rejection.
I break agreement with shame.
I receive truth.
I am Yours. I am whole. I am loved.

You Are Worth Loving

You were never meant to hate the person God loves. You were never meant to fear your own identity. You were never meant to apologize for existing.

The Father created you in His image. The Son redeemed you with His blood. The Spirit lives inside of you right now. So walk tall. Walk free. Walk clean. No more self-rejection. No more shame. No more punishment. You are healed. You are home. You are His.

Reflection Questions

1. In what ways have you rejected yourself — your appearance, calling, or story?

2. How has shame kept you from receiving love or celebrating who God made you to be?

3. What is one truth about your identity that you can speak over yourself daily?

12

FROM ORPHAN TO SON
EMBRACING SPIRITUAL ADOPTION

reedom from rejection is not just about healing the past—it's about stepping into a whole new identity. You weren't just rescued from sin. You weren't just delivered from spirits. You were adopted. You were brought into a family. Given a name. Filled with the Spirit. And placed in the Father's house—not as a servant, but as a son or daughter. This is the Spirit of adoption—the very heartbeat of the gospel. Until you receive it, you will always strive. But once you embrace it, you will finally rest.

From Orphanhood to Belonging

Romans 8:15 says:

"For you did not receive the spirit of slavery to fall back into fear, but you received the Spirit of adoption, by whom we cry, 'Abba! Father!'"
ESV

The orphan spirit says:

- "You're on your own."
- "You have to earn love."
- "You can't trust anyone."
- "There's not enough for you."
- "You better protect yourself."

But the Spirit of adoption says:

- "You belong."
- "You're loved before you perform."
- "You can trust Me."
- "There's an inheritance with your name on it."
- "You are safe."

The orphan spirit is the fruit of rejection. It makes you live like a slave. It makes you perform for love, compete for attention, and isolate when hurt. But sonship changes everything.

Sons Don't Strive—They Inherit

Galatians 4:7 says:

"You are no longer a slave, but a son; and if a son, then an heir through God." ESV

- Slaves live on assignment.
- Sons live from affection.
- Slaves work to be accepted.
- Sons work from being accepted.
- Sons know they have access.
- They know the house is theirs.
- They don't have to manipulate, compete, or prove.
- They already belong.

This is your inheritance—not one day in Heaven, but right now on Earth.

Jesus Lived as a Son

Jesus is our model for sonship. Before He performed a single miracle, the Father declared:

> *"This is My beloved Son, in whom I am well pleased." (Matthew 3:17) NKJV*

That identity grounded Jesus through:

- The wilderness (Matthew 4)
- The betrayal of friends
- The pressure of the crowd
- The brutality of the cross

The enemy came after His identity first: "If You are the Son of God..." But Jesus didn't need to prove anything—He knew who He was.

The same Spirit that lived in Him now lives in you. And that Spirit still cries out, "Abba! Father!"

What It Means to Be Adopted by God

Spiritual adoption isn't metaphorical—it's legal, relational, and irrevocable. Ephesians 1:5 says:

> *"He predestined us for adoption to sonship through Jesus Christ, in accordance with His pleasure and will." NIV*

Adoption means:

- You've been chosen—not tolerated.
- You've been brought in—not barely accepted.
- You carry the name and nature of your Father.
- You have access, authority, and identity.
- You are not a visitor—you are home.

The Characteristics of a Son (or Daughter)

1. Security

You no longer fear rejection. You know who you are. You don't need constant affirmation—you've already been affirmed by the only One who matters.

2. Access

You come boldly before God (Hebrews 4:16). You don't feel like an outsider in prayer. You approach your Father, not a boss.

3. Identity

You don't compare yourself to others. You don't chase titles or positions. You carry identity that isn't based on performance.

4. Rest

You don't strive to earn anything. You work from peace, not for approval. Your inner world is no longer in constant survival mode.

5. Inheritance

You believe blessing is your portion. You expect favor,

breakthrough, and legacy. You build for the future—because sons leave inheritance.

Healing the Orphan Spirit

To embrace adoption, you must renounce the orphan mindset:

"I break agreement with the orphan spirit. I reject the lie that I am on my own. I am not abandoned—I am adopted. I am not rejected—I am chosen. I am not striving—I am resting. I receive the Spirit of adoption and the love of the Father."

Then begin walking in it—practically, daily.

How to Walk in Sonship

1. Spend Time with the Father

Don't just do devotions—build connection. Let your prayer life be rooted in relationship, not routine. Ask Him, "Father, how do You see me today?"

2. Stop Performing

You don't have to earn your place. You already have it. Start doing things with God instead of just for God.

3. Embrace Correction as a Son

Hebrews 12:6 says:

> *"The Lord disciplines the one He loves." NIV*

Sons are corrected, not condemned. They grow because they know they're loved.

4. Receive Love—Even When You Feel Weak

You don't lose your status on bad days. The prodigal was still a son in the pigpen. God's love doesn't waver based on your emotions or performance.

5. Declare Sonship Daily

Wake up and say:

"I am a son. I am loved. I am secure. I belong. I am not alone. I am chosen."

Let the Spirit Cry Out

Romans 8:16 says:

"The Spirit Himself testifies with our spirit that we are children of God." NKJV

That cry—"Abba, Father!"—is the echo of adoption. Let the Spirit in you rise. Let the voice of rejection be silenced. Let the orphan mindset be broken. Let the Father love you.

You Belong in the House

You're not outside the door hoping to be noticed. You're not a servant in the shadows. You're not a hired hand trying to earn a place. You're family. You carry the Father's name. You wear the robe of righteousness. You sit at the table of grace. You are a son. You are a daughter. You are home. And no spirit of rejection will ever have the final say again.

Reflection Questions

1. What does it feel like to live as a spiritual orphan — always striving to belong?

2. What would it look like to live as a beloved son or daughter instead?

3. Ask the Father how He sees you. Write what He says.

PART III

LIVING AS ONE WHO IS LOVED

13

REBUILDING RELATIONSHIPS AFTER REJECTION

*H*ealing from rejection doesn't stop at freedom—it continues through connection. God never intended for healing to make you more independent. True healing makes you more capable of covenant. And yet, for many, even after they've walked through deliverance and embraced sonship, relationships still feel risky.

Why? Because rejection didn't just wound your heart—it rewired how you relate.

- You learned to protect instead of trust.
- To withhold instead of share.
- To control instead of connect.
- To survive instead of love.

This chapter is about learning how to rebuild relationships from a healed place—not by returning to old patterns, but by forming new ones rooted in honor, trust, vulnerability, and truth.

The Fallout of Rejection on Relationships

When you've been rejected, even unintentionally, your soul develops relational habits to survive:

- You assume people don't like you unless they prove it constantly.
- You shut down at the first sign of conflict.
- You read too deeply into tone, silence, and distance.
- You over-share to win approval or under-share to avoid pain.
- You fear intimacy, correction, or commitment.

These patterns are not evidence that you're "bad at relationships"—they're evidence of unhealed trauma. Now that the Spirit of adoption has come, these patterns must be confronted and replaced.

You Can't Heal in Isolation

Many people say things like:

- "It's just me and Jesus now."
- "I don't need people—I just need God."
- "I'm better off alone."

Those are orphan statements, not Kingdom ones. Yes, Jesus is enough to save you. But He designed the body of Christ to walk with you. Healing may begin in solitude, but it is completed in community. Romans 12:5 says:

"We, though many, are one body in Christ, and individually members one of another." ESV

You were not made for survival—you were made for family.

From Walls to Boundaries

After being rejected, many people build walls. But walls don't just keep danger out—they keep love out too. What you need is not walls but boundaries. Walls are built from fear:

- "No one gets in."
- "I'll never be vulnerable again."
- "If I feel exposed, I'll retreat."

Boundaries are built from wisdom:

- "Here's where access is healthy."
- "Here's how I communicate when I feel unsafe."
- "Here's what I need to feel protected while still staying open."

Boundaries are not rejection—they are protection for connection.

Building Relationships From a Healed Place

Let's walk through five key foundations for rebuilding healthy, godly relationships after rejection:

1. Identity-Based Connection

When you know who you are, you don't need others to constantly validate you. You can:

- Show up with confidence, not insecurity.
- Share without oversharing.

- Receive love without suspicion.
- Be honest without fearing rejection.

When your identity is rooted in sonship, your presence becomes a gift—not a demand.

2. Honest Vulnerability

Vulnerability is not weakness—it's strength that tells the truth. Ephesians 4:25 says:

"Therefore each of you must put off falsehood and speak truthfully to your neighbor, for we are all members of one body." NIV

Speak the truth about:

- What you feel
- What you need
- What triggers you
- What brings you joy
- What helps you feel safe

Vulnerability creates intimacy—but only when paired with wisdom. Trust must be earned and tested, but hiding can no longer be your default.

3. Communication That Builds Instead of Destroys

When you're used to being misunderstood, you often communicate defensively. But healed people learn how to:

- Listen without assumption
- Ask instead of accuse

- Clarify instead of control
- Own their feelings instead of blaming

Proverbs 15:1 says:

"A gentle answer turns away wrath, but a harsh word stirs up anger." NIV

Communication is not just about being heard—it's about building bridges.

4. Relearning Trust in Covenant Relationships

Trust is not given—it's built. And if rejection taught you to expect abandonment, rebuilding trust will feel like climbing a mountain. Start small:

- Trust people with your presence.
- Let someone pray for you.
- Ask for help without apologizing.
- Let others carry you when you're weak.

You don't need to trust everyone. But God will assign you to some who are trustworthy. Give them access. Test it over time. And walk in covenant, not just convenience.

5. Allowing God to Restore What Was Broken

Joel 2:25 says:

"I will restore to you the years that the locust has eaten..." NKJV

This includes relational years. God can:

- Heal your marriage
- Restore broken friendships
- Rebuild spiritual trust
- Renew hope for connection

You may have had toxic friendships or leaders in the past. But that doesn't mean you were made for isolation. You were made for family.

Forgive Again—This Time With Vision

Forgiveness isn't just for the past—it's also for your future. You can't build new relationships while carrying old bitterness. If rejection created deep betrayal or abandonment, choose to:

- Forgive the person again—as many times as needed (Matthew 18:22)
- Release them from your expectations
- Let God restore your capacity to love

Your ability to build healthy connection is tied to your willingness to release the weight of unhealthy ones.

Becoming a Safe Person for Others

Healing doesn't just make you want connection—it equips you to carry it. The goal isn't just to have better friends—it's to become a safe and healthy person in community. Ask yourself:

- Can people be weak around me without fear of judgment?
- Do I pursue clarity instead of assuming offense?
- Do I carry conversations with honor and truth?
- Do I speak life even when correcting?

You're not just healed for your sake—you're healed so others can find healing through you.

You Can Love Again—Deeply and Safely

Rejection told you that love was risky. Sonship tells you that love is your nature. You don't need to hide anymore. You don't need to shrink. You don't need to over-explain. You are loved. You are accepted. You are safe. And now, you can help others feel the same.

Let's Rebuild Together

You may have walked alone for years. You may have been hurt by people you trusted. You may have believed connection wasn't for you. But the Father is restoring your relational garden. He's teaching you how to be loved—and how to love again. Not perfectly—but purely. Not anxiously—but securely. So open the door again. Invite someone in. Let your life become a house of healing.

Reflection Questions

1. What relationship in your life needs rebuilding through grace and honesty?

2. How can you create safe, healthy connection without fear of being hurt again?

3. What step can you take this week to love someone without self-protection?

14

STAYING FREE AND ROOTED IN LOVE

*D*eliverance is powerful. Healing is beautiful. But freedom must be maintained. Jesus doesn't just want to set you free—He wants you to stay free, live free, and lead others into that freedom.

Many people walk through inner healing or deliverance and feel completely transformed... for a while. But weeks or months later, they feel the old insecurities creeping in. Old patterns begin resurfacing. New rejections trigger old wounds. The enemy whispers again, and they wonder, "Did I really change?"

Yes, you did. But freedom doesn't flourish without intentionality. Deliverance breaks the chain. But discipline keeps it off.

This chapter will show you how to cultivate a lifestyle that protects your freedom and reinforces your identity—so you never go back to the old lies.

Freedom Is a Daily Decision

Galatians 5:1 says:

"It is for freedom that Christ has set us free. Stand firm, then, and do not let yourselves be burdened again by a yoke of slavery." NIV

Freedom is not a one-time event. It's a daily stance. A daily choice. A daily stand. You must guard your heart, renew your mind, and stay rooted in God's love—or the lies you broke agreement with will attempt to return.

Why Old Patterns Try to Come Back

When the enemy is cast out, he looks for rest. Jesus said:

"When an unclean spirit goes out of a person... it returns to the house it left. If it finds it empty, it brings seven other spirits more wicked than itself." (Matthew 12:43–45) NIV

That's why post-deliverance life must be filled:

- With truth
- With the Holy Spirit
- With new thought patterns
- With strong boundaries
- With loving community

The devil doesn't need a new strategy—he just needs an open door.

Four Core Practices to Stay Free

Let's walk through the four daily habits that will help you

maintain your freedom, grow deeper in sonship, and silence rejection for good.

1. Daily Identity Declaration

You must declare truth louder than the enemy whispers lies. Declare over yourself each morning:

- "I am loved, accepted, and secure in the Father's heart."
- "I do not perform for approval—I live from identity."
- "I am not who I was—I am a new creation in Christ."
- "I am not rejected—I am accepted in the Beloved."

Don't just think truth—speak it. Out loud. Into the atmosphere. Words build strongholds—either demonic or divine. Choose truth.

2. Abide in the Word and Presence of God

You cannot stay free without abiding in the One who set you free. John 15:5 says:

"He who abides in Me, and I in him, bears much fruit; for without Me, you can do nothing." NKJV

Your identity is sustained by:

- The Word — You must replace the lies of the past with the truth of Scripture daily.
- Worship — Rejection cannot survive where love is exalted.

- Prayer — Stay in open conversation with your Father. Let Him affirm and align you daily.

Abiding is not about performance—it's about presence. It's where roots grow.

3. Recognize and Resist Triggers Early

Healing doesn't mean you'll never be triggered. It means you'll know how to respond when you are. Pay attention to moments when you feel:

- Suddenly insecure or anxious
- Easily offended or withdrawn
- Disconnected or emotionally numb
- Angry or defensive with no clear reason

Instead of reacting, ask:

"Father, is this an old pattern trying to re-enter?"

Then respond with truth:

"That's not who I am anymore. I'm a son. I'm safe. I'm seen. I'm secure."

Old triggers lose power when you meet them with new identity.

4. Stay Planted in Healthy Community

Rejection thrives in isolation. Sonship flourishes in family. You need people who:

- Remind you who you are when you forget
- Confront you in love when you drift
- Celebrate you without competition
- Pray with you through pain
- Walk with you into purpose

Hebrews 10:25 says:

> "Do not neglect meeting together, as some do, but encourage one
> another daily." NIV

You don't need perfect people—you need committed ones. Find them. Be one. Stay connected.

Replacing Religion With Relationship

One of the most deceptive returns of rejection is religious striving. After freedom, you may feel tempted to:

- Do more "for God" to stay qualified
- Earn intimacy through works
- Measure your worth by performance again

Resist this temptation. Jesus said in John 15:15:

> "I no longer call you servants... I call you friends." NIV

You don't need to impress God to keep His affection.
You already have it. Don't return to slavery in the name of spiritual growth. Stay rooted in grace.

Watch for These Sneaky Open Doors

Here are some subtle ways rejection tries to sneak back in:

- Overthinking after a conversation
- ("Did they think I was annoying?")
- Assuming people are mad or distant
- ("They didn't text—must be done with me.")
- Self-condemnation after a mistake
- ("I knew I'd mess this up again.")
- Obsessing over affirmation
- ("Why didn't they notice me?")
- Isolating when triggered
- ("I'll just disappear for a while.")

Catch the lie. Stop the spiral. Speak the truth.

Make Rest a Weapon

Slaves hustle. Sons rest. One of the most spiritual things you can do to stay free is to rest:

- Take a Sabbath.
- Turn off your phone.
- Enjoy God without an agenda.
- Let yourself be instead of always doing.

Psalm 46:10 says:

> *"Be still and know that I am God." NKJV*

Stillness anchors identity. Rest resets your soul. And joy becomes strength when it's not based on performance.

You Are Not Going Back

The enemy may try to whisper:

- "You'll fall again."
- "You're still the same."
- "Freedom never lasts."

But here's what you say back:

"I am not who I was. I am filled with the Spirit. I am rooted in love. I am walking in truth. I am surrounded by family. I am unshakeable, unafraid, and fully loved."

Rejection doesn't get a second chance. Fear doesn't get a foothold. Shame doesn't get a say. You are free, and you are staying free.

You Are Becoming Whole

- Every time you speak truth, a root grows deeper.
- Every time you resist a lie, your mind is renewed.
- Every time you receive love, your heart expands.
- Every time you show up, even when triggered, you build muscle.

This is the rhythm of wholeness. Not perfection—but presence. Not control—but trust. Not fear—but love. The more you stay rooted in love, the more fruit you'll bear. And nothing—not rejection, not failure, not opinion—can take that away.

Reflection Questions

1. What old patterns or lies still try to pull you back into rejection?

2. How can rest, stillness, and abiding in God's presence guard your freedom?

3. What daily rhythms help you stay rooted in love instead of striving for it?

15

YOU ARE CHOSEN, NOT FORSAKEN

*T*his is your declaration: You are not who rejection said you were. You are not forsaken. You are not forgotten. You are not unworthy. You are chosen. Chosen before the foundation of the world. Chosen in love. Chosen with purpose. Chosen for glory.

The lie of rejection has been broken. The orphan spirit has been cast out. The shame has been removed. The Spirit of adoption has come—and you are home. Now, it's time to live like it.

You Are Not on the Outside Anymore

For so long, rejection convinced you that you were:

- Always on the outside looking in
- Always second-best
- Always one mistake away from being discarded

But here's the truth: You're in the family. You're not an

outsider anymore. You're not the overlooked one. You are not the extra, the exception, or the afterthought. You are the beloved. The Father has set His affection on you. Jesus has clothed you in righteousness. The Spirit has sealed you with adoption. You belong here.

You Don't Need to Prove Anything Anymore

You don't need to earn love. You don't need to be "enough." You don't need to post, perform, or please to feel worthy. Because the cross has already spoken:

"It is finished."

That means your striving can cease. Your identity is not up for debate. Your value is not dependent on others. You are free from the cycle of performance. You are loved as you are— before you do anything else. That's grace. That's adoption. That's the Kingdom.

You Are Being Sent—Healed and Whole

You are not just healed for you—you're healed to become a healer. Jesus didn't rescue you from rejection just so you could feel better. He rescued you to send you:

- Into your family with new vision
- Into your church with restored love
- Into your workplace with authority
- Into your calling without shame

What once disqualified you has become your mantle. What once silenced you has become your voice. You are a carrier of the Father's heart now. And the world needs what you carry.

Rejected by Men, Chosen by God

1 Peter 2:4 says:

"As you come to Him, the living Stone—rejected by men but chosen by God and precious to Him..." NIV

Jesus was rejected so you never would be again. Now you stand in the same grace:

- Rejected by some, but chosen by God.
- Misunderstood by the world, but seen by Heaven.
- Passed over by man, but hand-picked by the Father.

You're not defined by who walked away. You're defined by who came running—Jesus.

The Mantle of the Beloved

You wear something new now.

- It's not rejection.
- It's not shame.
- It's not insecurity.
- It's sonship.
- You wear the robe of righteousness.
- You wear the signet ring of authority.
- You wear the sandals of peace.

You've come out of the pigpen, into the house, and now you carry the heart of the Father to others. Wherever you go, you release:

- Safety instead of suspicion

- Belonging instead of performance
- Love instead of fear
- Wholeness instead of chaos

This is your new identity: Beloved, anointed, accepted, and sent.

A Prophetic Commissioning

I declare over you—you are not forsaken. The voice of rejection is broken. The spirit of fear is evicted. The orphan mindset is over. The Father has claimed you, named you, and marked you as His own.

You are rising now—not to prove something, but because love has made you whole. You are stepping into boldness—not because you're fearless, but because you're secure. You are building covenant, releasing healing, and restoring others—not from striving, but from rest.

Where you once begged for scraps, you now prepare a table. Where you once performed for love, you now carry love. Where you once felt abandoned, you now call others home.

You are a son. You are a daughter. You are not who they said you were. You are not who rejection tried to make you. You are not stuck in old labels, lies, or limitations.

You are a new creation. You are marked by mercy. You are filled with the Spirit. You are accepted and free.

Final Words: Stay in the Father's Arms

You never graduate from sonship. You never outgrow the need to be loved by the Father. You never move on from the place of intimacy. Stay there. Abide there. Let His love remain the loudest voice. Because when love is louder than fear, When truth is louder than lies, When presence is deeper than pain— You won't just walk in freedom. You'll carry it into every room you enter.

Let the world say what it wants. Let the old wounds try to whisper. Let the enemy scheme. But your identity is settled:

You are chosen. You are not forsaken. You are free.

Reflection Questions

1. What truth from this book has most reshaped how you see yourself?

2. How does it feel to say out loud: "I am chosen, accepted, and free"?

3. What will living as a chosen son or daughter look like in your relationships, purpose, and future?

APPENDIX A

INNER HEALING PRAYER MODEL: PRESENTING JESUS IN MEMORY-BASED HEALING

This model helps you walk someone (or yourself) through a healing encounter where Jesus speaks truth into a moment of pain or trauma. It's not about psychological recall—it's about spirit-led restoration.

1. Identify

Ask the Holy Spirit to bring to mind the earliest or most painful memory connected to a specific lie, wound, or emotion.

> "Holy Spirit, what is the root of this feeling of rejection/fear/shame?"

2. Invite

Invite Jesus into the memory. He is not bound by time—He is present in the moment that wounded you.

> "Jesus, where were You in this moment?"

3. Listen

Pause and listen. Let Him show you something—His face, His presence, His words, or even how He felt about what happened.

4. Forgive

Walk through forgiving the people involved. Speak their names aloud. Forgiveness doesn't excuse them—it frees you.

> "I choose to forgive [name] for [action], and I release them to You."

5. Renounce

Break agreement with the lie you believed in that moment.

> "I break agreement with the lie that I'm unwanted/unworthy/alone."

6. Replace

Ask Jesus to give you His truth in place of the lie.

> "Jesus, what's the truth You want me to know?"

Receive it. Declare it. Write it down.

APPENDIX B

DELIVERANCE FROM THE SPIRIT OF REJECTION: PRAYER, RENUNCIATION, AND EVICTION OF COMPANION SPIRITS

Deliverance from rejection often includes breaking ties with other spirits that entered through trauma, fear, or prolonged agreement with lies. Use this process with humility, boldness, and full surrender.

1. Sample Prayer of Renunciation and Deliverance

In the name of Jesus, I renounce and break every agreement I made with the spirit of rejection. I cancel its right to influence my identity, my emotions, my decisions, and my relationships.

I also renounce every spirit connected to rejection, including fear, insecurity, shame, abandonment, pride, control, rebellion, self-hatred, depression, perfectionism, isolation, people-pleasing, striving, and the orphan spirit.

I command every unclean spirit to leave me now in the name of Jesus Christ. You have no place, no right, and no authority in my life.

Holy Spirit, fill every place that was emptied. Seal me in truth. I receive the Spirit of adoption. I am a beloved son/daughter of the Father. I am free, I am chosen, I am whole. Amen.

2. Common Companion Spirits to Evict with Rejection:

- Fear of man
- Abandonment
- Insecurity
- Shame
- Pride
- Control
- Rebellion
- Orphan spirit
- Bitterness
- Envy
- Victimhood
- Passivity
- Self-pity
- Self-hatred
- Depression
- Isolation
- Performance and striving
- Religious perfectionism

Speak them out and evict them one by one as led by the Holy Spirit.

3. Daily Declarations for Freedom and Sonship

Speak these aloud every morning for 30 days—or until they're your default mindset.

- "I am loved and accepted in the Beloved."
- "I belong in the Father's house."
- "I am not rejected—I am chosen."
- "I am not alone—God is with me and for me."
- "I don't perform for identity—I live from it."
- "I am safe in relationships because I am secure in Christ."
- "I walk in sonship, not striving."
- "I release fear and receive perfect love."
- "My voice matters, my life matters, and I have nothing to prove."
- "I am free from rejection forever."

APPENDIX C

SCRIPTURES FOR IDENTITY AND ACCEPTANCE: MEDITATE, MEMORIZE, AND DECLARE

Use these verses to rebuild the foundation of your identity in God.

- Ephesians 1:4–6 – "Chosen... predestined for adoption... accepted in the Beloved."
- Romans 8:15–17 – "You have received the Spirit of adoption... heirs of God."
- 1 Peter 2:9 – "You are a chosen people, a royal priesthood..."
- Galatians 4:6–7 – "Because you are sons, God has sent forth the Spirit of His Son into your hearts..."
- Isaiah 49:16 – "See, I have engraved you on the palms of My hands."
- Psalm 27:10 – "Though my father and mother forsake me, the Lord will receive me."
- Jeremiah 31:3 – "I have loved you with an everlasting love..."
- Zephaniah 3:17 – "He will rejoice over you with singing..."

- Hebrews 13:5 – "I will never leave you nor forsake you."
- John 15:15 – "I no longer call you servants... but friends."

APPENDIX D
10 SIGNS YOU'VE BEEN HEALED FROM REJECTION

Look for these signs as evidence of transformation. Use them for reflection, journaling, or discipleship.

1. Confidence in Identity
2. You no longer waver under pressure or comparison. You know who you are.
3. Emotional Stability
4. You respond, not react. Triggers don't spiral you into shame or fear.
5. Consistent Intimacy with God
6. You enjoy time with the Father instead of performing for Him.
7. Freedom from Performance
8. You do what you do out of love, not to earn love.
9. Ability to Receive Correction Without Collapse
10. You no longer interpret feedback as rejection.
11. Healthy Boundaries Without Walls
12. You know how to stay open without being vulnerable to destruction.

13. Covenant Relationships
14. You walk in deep, safe community where you are known, seen, and celebrated.
15. Freedom from People-Pleasing
16. You no longer compromise who you are to keep others happy.
17. Joy in Rest
18. You don't need to "earn" days off, love, or presence. You've learned to be, not just do.
19. Overflowing Love for Others
20. You've become a healer, not just a survivor. You now give what you once longed for.

This is the fruit of healing. This is the life of sonship. This is your inheritance. You are accepted. You are free. You are a beloved child of the Father.

ABOUT THE AUTHOR

Tom Cornell is the Senior Leader of SOZO Church in Washington state, founder of Walk in the Light International and SOZO Network. Tom is married to his beautiful wife Katy and lives in the Puget Sound area with her and their three kids. He has been in ministry pastoring and teaching the body of Christ since 2008.

He has a passion to see the body of Christ moving from people with an orphan mindset to that of sonship; equipping the body to do the work of Jesus resulting in seeing the Kingdom of God manifested here on earth.

www.ingramcontent.com/pod-product-compliance
Lightning Source LLC
Chambersburg PA
CBHW071029280326
41935CB00011B/1508